Take a gawk

Lawson Hanson

Contents

Chapter 1

Take a gander

In Australian slang the terms *"Take a gander"* and *"Take a gawk"* mean much the same — *"Take a look at this"* or *"Examine this"* or *"Inspect this"* or these — objects, or ideas, or concepts that somebody wants to show us.

In the Linux computer world the term 'gawk' represents the *mnemonic* command name of the GNU version of the AWK interpreter and gets described as a:

pattern scanning and processing language

AWK started life around 1977 — during the development of the Unix computer operating system at AT&T Bell Labs.

My guess is AWK got its name from the family name initials of its three co-authors — Alfred V. Aho, Brian W. Kernighan and Peter J. Weinberger.

These developers of the AWK interpreter published a book titled: *"The AWK Programming Language"* in 1988 — a clear and concise publication with about 210 pages — well worth the read if we can find that somewhere.

It describes an extremely powerful tool that can get put into service in countless ways to solve problems involving the validation, manipulation and formatting of data.

On pages 17 and 18 of their book the authors list twenty examples in a section titled: **A Handful of Useful "One-liners"** to display the power of the language to perform actions of some complexity with one or two simple statements. For example:

Print the last field on each input line:

```
{ print $NF }
```

Print every line with more than four fields:

```
NF > 4
```

Print the number of fields on each input line followed by the entire line of data itself:

```
{ print NF, $0 }
```

I get amazed at something else I discover AWK has been able to do for decades — every time I browse among the pages of their fascinating book.

The language has a syntax that's similar to that of the C programming language, and although it's an interpreted language, it performs at good speed due to its in-built string handling capability.

Why should we want to look at a programming language that (in 2025) is almost half a century old?

AWK is an expressive language — we find useful programs can get written in one or two or three (often *short*) lines of code — more over, it can get used to produce elegant solutions to far more complex tasks.

When writing complicated programs the AWK interpreter is indispensable for helping with the task of prototyping — in particular because we can experiment with small fragments of code and use the Linux shell pipe ('|') mechanism to help connect the standard output of one fragment into the standard input of the next fragment — making pipelines of AWK and interspersed Linux command(s) — almost ad-infinitum.

For another reason — most of the bugs got eradicated long ago. A bug free program will continue to do what it got designed to do — time — after time — after time.

I appreciate solid reliability.

To me — AWK is amazing — it's worth more than its weight in gold and in my consideration it's Use-By Date is nowhere close to reaching *"expired."*

Most of the information processing I need to do involves files containing plain text or data values like numbers or strings of text — separated by blank spaces or another *field* separator character — punctuation symbols or another pre-defined character code.

Each statement in an AWK program gets composed from two *optional* parts:

1. A pattern — to locate line items of interest

2. An action — to run on the matching data

The primary activity performed by AWK is to read a series of input data lines — one after another — searching for lines that get matched by any of the *pattern(s)* we specify and then taking the associated *action(s)* we choose to define.

It's usual to write AWK statements like this:

    pattern { *action* }
    pattern { *action* }

We enclose the *"action"* part(s) within curly brace characters ('{ ... }') to distinguish those from the *"pattern"* part(s) we write.

We need to specify one and/or the other of those parts — they can't both get left undefined — at times one part can.

AWK will scan each line of input (from its *standard input* or from another specified file) looking for matches to a *pattern* (if specified) — and take the appropriate *action* (if this part got specified).

If we don't define any *pattern* part then the *action* gets run on *every* line of input data while the script runs.

If we don't specify any *action* part then the default *action* is to `print` the line(s) that *match* the *pattern*.

Note: An empty pair of curly braces ({ }) is **not** an *unspecified action* — it represents a 'do-nothing' *action* — not always what we want or expected.

If all we need to do is ignore lines that match a specified *pattern* a better way to do that is to use a special *action* called 'next':

    pattern { next }

AWK uses meta-characters — like curly-braces, square brackets, dollar symbols and others — that also get used by the Linux shells (like 'bash').

To hide these meta-characters from the shell — either on a command-line or within a bash shell script — we will generally *surround* the AWK code by using a *pair* of right single quote characters: ('...{ ...}').

Using these (as we must needs do) means it's difficult to use
that (') character within an AWK program — bear that in
mind — it's not impossible.

We could define a variable named like 'rsq' (mnemonic for
right single quote) with the value of the ASCII character
code for that (') character: (Octal: 047; Decimal: 39; or
Hexadecimal: "0x27").

We can use that in conditional tests and function calls
or write it out with a ("%c") character format string in a
'printf' statement like this:

```
$ echo | awk '{ rsq = 39
printf "Output rsq:   (%c) \n", rsq }' -
Output rsq:   (')
```

Piping (|) the empty 'echo' command into the 'awk' process
provides one blank line of input (a single *newline* character)
upon which AWK can perform the specified *action* — a
convenient way to test snippets of code.

Using the right single quote (') characters to define the limits
of our AWK program brings with it the added benefit that
we can write longer bits of AWK code on more than one line
— this is a feature of the shell meta-characters that I find
most helpful.

The AWK interpreter will continue reading and parsing and
interpreting the code we write until it finds the *next* closing
right single quote character — like I have shown in that two
line example. The third line shows its output.

Let's use the Linux 'ncal' command to supply a sample of
input data lines:

```
$ ncal
     October 2025
  Su     5 12 19 26
```

```
Mo      6 13 20 27
Tu      7 14 21 28
We   1  8 15 22 29
Th   2  9 16 23 30
Fr   3 10 17 24 31
Sa   4 11 18 25
```

The '`ncal`' program lets us specify the month and year numbers — and we could run any of:

```
ncal 10 2025
ncal 1 2026
ncal 5 2026
ncal 7 2026
ncal 10 2026
ncal 1 2027
...
ncal 3 2030
```

to get a similar set of data showing a month with five (5) Fridays.

To print the record (*line*) number followed by the value of the first argument found on each line and then the number of fields counted on each line of the '`ncal`' output we can use an AWK command with one *action* and no *pattern* part. The *action* will get run on every line of input:

```
$ ncal | awk '{ print NR, $1, NF }' -
1 October 2
2 Su 5
3 Mo 5
4 Tu 5
5 We 6
6 Th 6
7 Fr 6
8 Sa 5
```

In the command-line above we *pipe* ('|') the *standard* output from the 'ncal' process into the *standard* input of 'awk'.

The hyphen or dash (-) character at the end of that command line specifies to AWK that it should read its input from the *standard input* stream — like when we piped in an empty 'echo' command in my 'rsq' example.

We can replace that dash with the name of a file if we want AWK to read from a saved text data file.

AWK reads a line of input and splits that into *fields* that it finds separated by blank characters — or other field separator characters we can define at run time if we need to.

AWK contains special variables like 'NF' for the number of fields (on the current input line) and 'NR' for the record number (of the current input line) — and '$1' provides the *value* of the first field (on the current input line).

The NF variable gets set to the number of such fields that the AWK interpreter finds on each input line as it reads those — one by one.

A common Linux command we can use to extract the line that contains the Friday dates from the output of 'ncal' is:

```
$ ncal | grep 'Fr'
Fr   3 10 17 24 31
```

Here we pipe (|) the output of the 'ncal' command into the 'grep' command (its name is *mnemonic* for "*get regular expression and print*") looking for lines that contain the text string (or *pattern*) 'Fr' and it returns the one line that matches.

See 'man grep' for more information.

A Linux command line to run an AWK program to extract the line that contains the Friday dates from the output of 'ncal' is:

```
$ ncal | awk '/Fr/' -
Fr   3 10 17 24 31
```

Here I have used one form of an AWK *pattern* (`/Fr/`) — a
regular-expression constant enclosed between forward-slash
(`/`) characters without specifying any *action* — the *default*
action will `print` the matching input data line(s).

The output is the same as the '`grep`' command.

Then why not use '`grep`'?

What if we want to perform an *action* on that line of data?

Imagine we have a standing agreement with our work
colleagues to go out to lunch for an hour on the last Friday
in each month of the year that has five (5) Fridays. We would
get to do that about four times each year — some years five
— not too often to annoy the management gurus — make
sure to invite them — they're people too.

We can use AWK to help us announce when those events will
occur:

```
$ ncal | awk '/Fr/ { if (NF == 6)
    print "Luncheon day Friday", $NF}' -
Luncheon day Friday 31
```

The AWK *action* code in the example above consists of a
conditional '`if`' statement to test when the '`NF`' variable —
the number of fields in the current line of data is equal to '6'
and then a '`print`' statement with two comma (`,`) separated
arguments — a double (`"`) quoted string and '`$NF`' — to get
run when that *condition* is true.

The '`$NF`' part extracts the *value* of the *last* field on any
input line that matches the '`/Fr/`' *pattern*.

In reality we might like to do more with the emitted
information — like send email reminders to a list of names
and/or prompt somebody to make a restaurant booking?

AWK can help us with those tasks, too.

To read more about the 'gawk' interpreter and the programming language it encapsulates, we can use the 'man' command:

```
man gawk
```

The last time I checked this had over 2150 lines of documentation information. Using a Linux pager like the one called 'less' allows us to read the 'man' pages and search through them for *keywords* like the 'NF' variable names and for more details about the *"pattern"* and *"action"* parts.

On my Linux system the command names 'awk' and 'gawk' are synonymous and they both point to '/usr/bin/gawk' — the GNU version of AWK.

If we have input data that uses field separators other than blank characters we can use a command-line option ('-F') and an argument to tell AWK what to use.

For example, to extract the list of (colon ':' separated) items in our bash shell's PATH variable we could use this:

```
echo $PATH | awk -F':' '{
for (i=1; i<=NF; i++) { print $i } }' -
/usr/local/bin
/usr/sbin
/usr/bin
/sbin
/bin
/snap/bin
/usr/local/games
/usr/games
```

Here I have used a 'for' loop to iterate over each field — from 1 to NF and use a 'print' statement to display each of those fields on a separate line.

The '`for`' loop control *syntax* is like what we use in the programing languages '`C`' and '`C++`'.

The variable '`i`' gets initialized to '`1`' and then gets incremented by the '`i++`' part while its value is less than or equal to '`NF`'.

The successive '`print`' statements will look like: '`print $1`'; '`print $2`'; '`print $3`'; '`print $4`'; ...; for each of the colon ('`:`') separated *fields* that AWK finds in its input.

Chapter 2

AWK features

The AWK system includes a large set of *features* to help
make writing useful scripts and programs both easy and more
productive.

AWK contains a collection of useful internal functions we can
call to help us manipulate text strings and numbers and print
the results we choose to select from the lines of input our
AWK scripts read.

In the following sections we'll take a look at lists of
features such as 'operators', 'control statements',
'i/o statements', 'arithmetic functions' and 'string
functions'.

In later chapters we'll look at how to make use of some of
these feature ingredients of AWK.

2.1   Operators

The AWK system *operators* includes a list for tasks including
those that fall into the following categories: '*control,*' '*field
access,*' '*arithmetic,*' '*string,*' '*relational,*' '*logical,*' and

'assignment.'

;	—	semi-colon statement separator
(...)	—	parentheses for *grouping*
$	—	dollar symbol for *field reference*
++	—	*increment*
--	—	*decrement*
^ or **	—	*exponentiation operators*
!	—	*logical negation*
*	—	*multiplication*
/	—	*division*
%	—	*modulus* or *remainder*
+	—	*addition*
-	—	*subtraction*
space	—	blank space for *string concatenation*
< >	—	*relational operators*
<= >=	—	*relational operators*
== !=	—	*relational operators*
~ !~	—	*regular expression matching operators*
	—	*don't use a reg-ex constant (/.../)*
	—	*on the left-hand side of either of these*
in	—	*array membership*
&&	—	*logical AND*
||	—	*logical OR*
=	—	*assignment operators*
+= --=	—	*assignment operators*
*= /=	—	*assignment operators*
%= ^=	—	*assignment operators*

2.2 Control statements

The action coding flow control statements we can use in
AWK programs include these:

$\underline{\{\ \textit{statements}\ \}}$

— statement grouping

$\underline{\texttt{if}\ (\textit{condition})\ \textit{statement}}$

— if *condition* is true then execute *statement*

$\underline{\texttt{if}\ (\textit{condition})\ \textit{stmnt1}\ \texttt{else}\ \textit{stmnt2}}$

— if *condition* is true then execute *stmnt1*

— otherwise execute *stmnt2*

$\underline{\texttt{while}\ (\textit{condition})\ \textit{statement}}$

— if *condition* is true then execute *statement*

— and repeat while the *condition* remains true

$\underline{\texttt{for}\ (\textit{expr1}\ ;\ \textit{expr2}\ ;\ \textit{expr3})\ \textit{statement}}$

— equivalent to *expr1* ; followed by

— `while` (*expr2*) { *statement* ; *expr3* }

$\underline{\texttt{for}\ (\textit{var}\ \texttt{in}\ \textit{array})\ \textit{statement}}$

— execute *statement* with *var* set to

— each element in *array* in turn

$\underline{\texttt{do}\ \textit{statement}\ \texttt{while}\ (\textit{condition})}$

— execute *statement* ; if *condition* is true

— then repeat

$\underline{\texttt{break}}$

— exit the inner-most enclosing loop

— 'while', 'for' or 'do'

$\underline{\texttt{continue}}$

— commence next iteration of the innermost

— enclosing 'while', 'for' or 'do' loop

$\underline{\texttt{delete}\ \textit{array}\ [\textit{index}]}$

— delete the specified element at array[index]

```
delete array
```
— delete the entire specified array

```
next
```
— begin next iteration of the main input loop
— read next input data line if any; otherwise
— jump to the 'END' *action* if defined

```
exit
```
— jump to the 'END' *action* if defined
— otherwise exit the program

```
exit expression
```
— jump to the 'END' *action* if defined
— if already in the END action
— then exit the program with *expression*
— as the exit status value

```
switch (expression) {
    case value/regex : statement
    ...
    [ default:  statement ]
}
```
— use *expression* to match a **case**
— and run the corresponding *statement*
— otherwise run the **default** *statement*
— if that got defined

2.3   I/O statements

AWK has a series of input/output statements to help get
data into and out from our AWK scripts in different ways:

```
close("expression")
```
— close the specified file or pipe

<u>getline</u>
— update $0 from the next input line
— sets NF, NR and NFR

<u>getline <*file*</u>
— update $0 from the next input line from *file*
— sets NF

<u>getline *var*</u>
— set *var* from next input line
— sets NR and NFR

<u>getline *var* <*file*</u>
— set *var* from next input line from *file*

<u>*command* | getline *[var]*</u>
— run *command* and pipe the output
— into $0 or *var* if specified

<u>next</u>
— stop processing the current input record.
— read the next input record, if any, and
— start re-processing from the first *pattern*

<u>print</u>
— print the current input record

<u>print *expr-list*</u>
— print the items in *expr-list*

<u>print *expr-list* >*file*</u>
— print the items in *expr-list* out to *file*

<u>printf *fmt, expr-list*</u>
— print formatted *expt-list* items

printf *fmt, expr-list >file*
— print formatted *expt-list* items out to *file*

system("*cmd-line*")
— execute '*cmd-line*' and return exit status

See 'man gawk' for details of the flexible format specifiers the
printf statement can accept.

2.4 Arithmetic Functions

The AWK system contains built-in arithmetic functions
including:

sin(x)
— *sine of x with x in radians*

cos(x)
— *cosine of x with x in radians*

atan2(y, x)
— *arctangent of y/x in the range*
— *minus pi to plus pi*

exp(x)
— *exponential function of x*

log(x)
— *natural base e logarithm of x*

int(x)
— *integer part of x*

sqrt(x)
— *square root of x*

<u>rand()</u>
— *random floating point number*
— *between 0 and 1 inclusively*

<u>srand(x)</u>
— *specify that x is the new seed for* rand()

2.5   String Functions

Another area in which AWK excels is that of string handling.
AWK includes string manipulation functions such as these:

<u>gsub(r,s)</u>
— substitute string 's' for strings that match
— 'r' globally across the current line ('$0')
— returns the number of substitutions made

<u>gsub(r,s,t)</u>
— substitute 's' for 'r' globally in string 't'
— and return the number of substitutions

<u>index(s,t)</u>
— return first position of string 't' in 's'
— or 0 if 't' is not present in 's'

<u>length(s)</u>
— return number of characters in string 's'
— return number of elements in an array

<u>match(s,r)</u>
— test if 's' contains a substring matched
— by 'r' and return its *index* or 0;
— sets variables 'RSTART' and 'RLENGTH'

split(s,a)

— splits 's' into array 'a' using
— the *default* field separator 'FS'
— and return the number of fields

split(s,a,fs)

— splits 's' into array 'a' using
— the field separator 'fs' and
— return the number of fields

sprintf(fmt,expr-list)

— return 'expr-list' formatted with
— the format specifier string 'fmt'

strtonum(str)

— return the numeric value of 'str'.
— If 'str' begins with a leading '0x' or
— '0X', treat it as a Hexadecimal number.
— If 'str' begins with a leading '0'
— then treat it as an Octal number.
— Otherwise, treat it as a Decimal number.

sub(r,s)

— substitute 's' for the left-most longest
— substring of '$0' matched by 'r' and
— return the number of substitutions made

sub(r,s,t)

— substitute 's' for the left-most longest
— substring of 't' matched by 'r' and
— return the number of substitutions made

substr(s,p)

— return the suffix of string 's'
— starting at position 'p'

`substr(s,p,n)`
— return substring of 's' with length 'n'
— starting at position 'p'

`tolower(str)`
— return a copy of 'str' with all the
— UPPERCASE characters translated
— into `lowercase` characters

`toupper(str)`
— return a copy of 'str' with all the
— `lowercase` characters translated
— into UPPERCASE characters

Chapter 3

More features

Earlier I used one or two small 'pattern { action }' lines
to get AWK to extract simple data elements from its input.

The AWK *"pattern"* part (or parts) can include two fixed
patterns called 'BEGIN' and 'END' — and can take other forms
as described below.

3.1   AWK pattern forms

1. *BEGIN* { *statements* }

   The *statements* get executed once *before*
   any line of input data gets read — a good
   place to initialize variables or to print report
   header text and other such tasks

2. *END* { *statements* }

   The *statements* get executed once *after* all
   the input data gets read — a good place to
   print data totals or a process summary and
   write out report footer information

   Note: when the AWK interpreter meets
   an 'exit' command in an END action the

program will exit back to its caller

3. *expression* { *statements* }

   The *statements* get executed for each line
   of input data where the *expression* is true
   (non-zero, non-null)

4. */regular expression/* { *statements* }

   The *statements* get executed for each line of
   input data containing a string of text that
   matches the *regular expression*

   The characters *backslash, circumflex, dollar,
   full-stop, left-* and *right- square* brackets,
   the *pipe* symbol, *left-* and *right- parentheses,
   asterisk, plus* symbol and *question* mark are
   meta-characters

5. *compound pattern* { *statements* }

   The *statements* get executed for each line of
   input data where the *compound pattern* is
   true (non-zero, non-null)

   A *compound pattern* can combine '**&&**' (**AND**),
   '**||**' (**OR**) and '**!**' (**NOT**) operators and can use
   '**(   )**' grouping parentheses

6. *pattrn1 ? pattrn2 : pattrn3* { *statements* }

   If *pattrn1* is true then AWK uses *pattrn2*
   otherwise AWK will use *pattrn3* to further
   test for cases where *statements* will get run.

   One or the other of the second or third
   patterns will get evaluated — not both.

   The ?: *operator* works like it does in C.

7. *pattern1, pattern2* { *statements* }

   The *statements* get executed for each line of
   input data from when *pattern1* gets matched,
   through to when *pattern2* gets matched

   This enables us to perform *actions* on an
   inclusive *range* of input data

8. When the interpreter meets an 'exit'
   command, program control gets transferred
   to the 'END' *pattern* if it got defined

3.2   Regular Expressions

The AWK system permits us to use a whole range of *'regular expressions'* characters and symbols to construct the *patterns* we want it to match in our input data.

These *regular expressions* are almost identical to those we can use with the 'egrep' command in Linux. The 'man' page for 'gawk' contains an entire section headed 'Regular Expressions' with detailed explanations about how to construct flexible patterns to find almost anything in our data.

If you have experience using the 'grep' or 'egrep' Linux tools you should find it comfortable working with AWK *regular expressions*.

If you are new to these ideas it can take a bit of practise to get the hang of them — after a while they start to make sense and they open up powerful programming paradigms.

In one of my first examples in this book I used a regular expression *'constant'* (the *pattern* '/Fr/') to help extract the 'Fr' (*'Friday'*) line of data from the 'ncal' command:

```
$ ncal | awk '/Fr/' -
Fr   3 10 17 24 31
```

Regular expressions can be more flexible than that.

In the table that follows 'c' is a character; 'r' is a *regular expression*; and 'm' and 'n' are small integer numbers for repetition counts of an 'r'.

Regular expressions get composed from characters and
meta-characters including these:

c	—	Matches the non-meta-character c
\c	—	Matches the literal character c
.	—	Matches any character including a newline
^	—	Matches the beginning of a string
$	—	Matches the end of a string
[abc...]	—	A character list: matches any of the characters 'abc....'
	—	You can include a range of characters by separating them with a dash.
	—	To include a literal dash in the list, put it first or last
[^abc...]	—	A negated character list: matches any character except 'abc....'
r1|r2	—	Alternation: matches either 'r1' or 'r2'
r1r2	—	Concatenation: matches 'r1', and then 'r2'
r+	—	Matches one or more of 'r'
r*	—	Matches zero or more of 'r'
r?	—	Matches zero or one of 'r'
(r)	—	Grouping: matches 'r'
r{m}	—	Numbers inside braces indicate repetition counts
	—	A single number in the braces means the regular expression 'r' gets repeated 'm' times.
r{m,}	—	A number followed by a comma means 'r' gets repeated at least 'm' times.
r{m,n}	—	Two numbers separated by a comma means 'r' gets repeated from 'm' to 'n' times

There are other special character pairs to match the beginnings and ends of strings and there is a whole series of character classes that describe entire lists of characters — for example:

`[:alnum:]` — Alphanumeric characters.
`[:alpha:]` — Alphabetic characters.
`[:blank:]` — Space or tab characters.
`[:cntrl:]` — Control characters.
`[:digit:]` — Numeric characters.
`[:lower:]` — Lowercase alphabetic characters.
`[:upper:]` — Uppercase alphabetic characters.

and others. See 'man gawk' for more details.

3.3   AWK's own variables

Another feature of AWK is that it maintains a collection of internal variables. We have already seen 'NF' and 'NR'. Here is a list describing those and others:

- ARGC

  number of arguments on the command-line

- ARGV

  array of arguments from the command-line

- FILENAME

  name of the *current* input file

- FNR

  record number in the *current* input file

- FS

  input field separator (*a blank space*)

- NF

  number of fields in the current input record

- NR

  number of input records the program has read

- OFMT

  output format for numbers ('%.6g')

- OFS

  output field separator (*a blank space*)

- ORS

  output record separator (*newline*)

- RLENGTH

  length of string matched by the '`match`' function

- RS

  input record separator

- RSTART

  start of string matched by the '`match`' function

- SUBSEP

  subscript separator (ASCII '`FS`' character)
  (character code is: Octal: 034; Dec: 28; Hex: 1C)

The GNU version of AWK ('`gawk`') maintains even more than these. See the section named *"Built-in Variables"* in the '`man gawk`' pages for more details.

3.4   Command line arguments

If we need to gain access to the command-line arguments
that get used to run an AWK script those first two variables
— 'ARGC' and 'ARGV' can provide what we need:

```
# File:   ca.awk --> Print the
#         command-line arguments
#         and input with or w/out
#         their NR record numbers
# Usage:
#    awk -f ca.awk [p=1] [-] [infl(s)]
BEGIN {
    printf "Cmd-Line-Args:"
    printf " %s", ARGV[1]
    for (i=2; i<ARGC; i++)
        printf " %s", ARGV[i]
    print ""
}
{ if (p>0) printf "%s ", NR ; print }
```

The items surrounded by square brackets ('[...]') on
the 'Usage:' line indicate these are optional — although one
of '-' or an input file will be needed.

I have a small sample input file called 'a.txt' that contains
these lines displayed by 'cat':

```
$ cat a.txt
line 1 in a.txt
line two
line 3
```

Running that AWK script with a selection of arguments
including *both* a '-' and my file name produces:

```
$ echo "look" | awk -f ca.awk p=1 - a.txt
```

```
Cmd-Line-Args:  p=1 - a.txt
1  look
2  line 1 in a.txt
3  line two
4  line 3
```

Notice the '-f ca.awk' part of the command line does not
get found in the 'ARGV' array — that was an '-opt/arg' to
the AWK interpreter itself and gets stripped out early in
the process — when it needs to find out what AWK code it's
supposed to interpret.

The 'p=1' argument sets the variable named 'p' to the value
'1' for use in our AWK code.

Look at the last line of the listing of 'ca.awk' — it tests if
variable 'p' is greater than zero ('0') to signify that we want
the record numbers ('NR') printed at the start of each output
line.

In the output listed above we see that the condition tested
true and the four lines printed by the last action line did
display those record numbers.

Line 1 came from the 'echo "look"' command piped into the
standard input stream; then came the three input lines from
the small test file 'a.txt'.

Rearranging the command-line arguments a little produces an
interesting result:

```
$ echo look | awk -f ca.awk a.txt p=5 -
Cmd-Line-Args:  a.txt p=5 -
line 1 in a.txt
line two
line 3
4  look
```

The position of the 'p=5' argument on the command line —

after the input file name — does not get evaluated by AWK until *after* it reads that input.

The trailing '-' (read from standard input indicator) will get AWK to look at that input stream *next* and because the value of 'p' is now greater than zero we see the record number ('NR') gets printed on the 'look' line from the 'echo' input.

AWK reads input from the specified files in the order we request.

The 'NR' variable get incremented in AWK for every line it reads — no matter what the source. The 'FNR' variable is a file specific counter for the current input file — if we needed that instead.

3.5   User variables

Variables in AWK can contain floating point numbers and text strings — no need to pre-define which.

The value in a variable can get re-assigned ('=') to anything else and/or coerced from one type to another.

To coerce a number to become a string — use the (blank space) string concatenation operator: (`var ""`) to append a null string (`""`).

To coerce a string to become a number — use the addition operator to add zero (`var + 0`).

```
number = string + 0
string = number ""
```

The numeric value of a string is the longest prefix part of the string that is numeric in content — plus/minus symbol(s), digits, decimal point and/or scientific ('e') number notation.

```
$ echo | awk '{
    cm = "1.e-2 metre"
    print "str.value:", cm
    if ((cm+0) == 0.01) {
        print "num.value:", (cm+0)
    } else {
        print "values not equal"
    }
}' -
str.value:  1.e-2 metre
num.value:  0.01
```

AWK will recognise any of the following number forms as decimal numbers with a value of five:

```
5 5.0 +5 5e0 0.5E+1 50e-1 005
```

Adding '0' to these values coerces them to the number 5:

```
$ str="5 5.0 +5 5e0 0.5E+1 50e-1 005"
$ echo $str | awk '{
    for (i=1; i<=NF; i++)
        print $i, "plus zero:", $i+0
}' -
5 plus zero:  5
5.0 plus zero:  5
+5 plus zero:  5
5e0 plus zero:  5
0.5E+1 plus zero:  5
50e-1 plus zero:  5
005 plus zero:  5
```

3.6   AWK arrays

Arrays are interesting items in AWK. These are known as "*associative*" arrays — indexed by string instead of numbers.

Unlike other programming languages — in AWK it's not
necessary to pre-specify the number of elements we want to
have in our array(s).

These spring into existence as and when we use them and do
not need to get assigned in any particular order.

Although AWK arrays are one-dimensional objects — it's
possible to *simulate* multi-dimensional arrays with the string
subscripts we use for them.

On page 52 of *"The AWK Programming Language"*,
the authors gave an example for the simulation of a
two-dimension array.

Here's my attempt at a 3D array:

```
for (i=1; i<=3; i++)
   for (j=1; j<=4; j++)
      for (k=1; k<=5; k++)
         arr[i, j, k] = 0
```

The result is an array with 60 elements (3 by 4 by 5) with
subscripts like '1,1,1', '1,1,2', '1,1,3', etc.

Internally these subscripts get stored as:

```
'1 SUBSEP 1 SUBSEP 1',
'1 SUBSEP 1 SUBSEP 2',
'1 SUBSEP 1 SUBSEP 3', etc.
```

This information comes in handy if ever we need access to
the array subscript values while stepping through all the
elements of an array.

3.7   A live example

The following example uses that simulated 3D array and
populates the elements with pseudo-random numbers to
provide real data for an experiment:

```
echo | awk '{
  srand(systime())
  for (i=1; i<=3; i++)
    for (j=1; j<=4; j++)
      for (k=1; k<=5; k++)
        arr[i, j, k] = rand()
  n = 0
  for (ndx in arr) {
    n++
    if (arr[ndx] > 0.95) {
      split(ndx, sbs, SUBSEP)
      print sbs[1], sbs[2], sbs[3],
        arr[ndx], n,
        arr[sbs[1], sbs[2], sbs[3]]
    }
  }
}
END {
  print 9, 9, 9, "array elements:", n
}' -
```

The output could be:

```
3 2 5 0.990073 8 0.990073
1 4 4 0.990909 17 0.990909
3 3 1 0.977212 19 0.977212
1 1 4 0.965673 37 0.965673
1 2 1 0.968171 44 0.968171
9 9 9 array elements:  60
```

Note The array elements might not get returned in the index order we expect — we could pipe this output through 'sort' if we wanted more order in the first three columns.

We could need to pad the index numbers in the first three columns of the output with leading zero values if they were longer than single digit numbers — if we did want to sort those lines by array index order.

In the chunk of code above I use the 'systime()' function that returns the system time in seconds since:

1970-01-01 00:00:00 UTC — the Unix Epoch

This gets a number to use in 'srand()' as the starting seed for the calls to 'rand()' used to populate the 3D array as it gets constructed in the first three nested 'for' loops.

The next 'for' loop uses the AWK 'in' operator to access every array element index ('arr[ndx]') that got populated in the simulated 3D array.

After incrementing a counter 'n++' — if the *value* of the current array element ('arr[ndx]') is greater than 0.95 then it makes a call to 'split(ndx, sbs, SUBSEP)' to separate the array index ('ndx') into a small (three element) array named 'sbs' (short for *subscripts*) to provide the three subscript numbers 'sbs[1]', 'sbs[2]' and 'sbs[3]'.

The 'print' statement displays the array index subscript numbers and the value it finds in the array at 'arr[ndx]' with the index 'ndx' and its array element access counter value, 'n'.

The second floating point number on each output line — in column six (6) shows that using the comma-separated subscript values with:

```
arr[sbs[1], sbs[2], sbs[3]]
```

does gain access to the same simulated 3D array elements
as those found at 'arr[ndx]' — because the numbers in
columns 4 and 6 are the same.

Note: Running this script manually about ten or fifteen
times I observed results ranging from as low as one (1)
through to eight (8) of the sixty (60) array elements that got
populated with a value greater than 0.95 — by my reckoning
that's:

```
60 * (1.0 - 0.95) = 3.00
```

on average plus or minus two or three standard deviations.

Another run gave:

```
3 2 3 0.990883 6 0.990883
2 3 1 0.960447 9 0.960447
2 3 5 0.957939 13 0.957939
3 3 1 0.976702 19 0.976702
1 1 4 0.977233 37 0.977233
2 1 5 0.952068 43 0.952068
3 1 2 0.988393 50 0.988393
1 3 1 0.997368 59 0.997368
9 9 9 array elements: 60
```

The AWK 'rand()' function appears to work well for general
"random number" application.

As a more rigorous test I ran the random value filled
array process 1000 times to count the array elements that
contained values over 0.95 in each run.

For convenience I had encapsulated the original twenty (20)
lines of AWK code for the random value filled simulated
3D array process into a bash shell *wrapper* that I named
'sim3d-arr-awk.sh'.

The one necessary addition in 'sim3d-arr-awk.sh' was a
Linux bash shell 'hash-bang-bin-bash' line at the top before
the first line of that AWK code:

```
#!/usr/bin/bash
echo | awk '{
  srand(systime())
  ...
}
END {
  print 9, 9, 9, "array elements:", n
}' -
```

I used the following piece of interactive bash shell code from
my command line:

```
$ time for i in $(seq 0 999) ; do
>    sleep 1.2
>    ./sim3d-arr-awk.sh | awk '{n++}
>      END { print n-1 }' -
> done | awk '{c[$1]++}
>    END {for (s in c) print s, c[s]}' -
```

Using the Linux 'time' command to report on the time
taken by the experiment that uses the 'seq' (*sequence*)
command to generate 1000 numbers from 0 to 999 to give
the 'for-do-done' loop an iteration stepping list of values.

The fractional 'sleep 1.2' process between each iteration of
the loop means that the process should take:

```
1000 * 1.2 = 1200 seconds
```

— or about 20 minutes to run.

Piping the output of 'sim3d-arr-awk.sh' into another bit of
AWK code counts the number of lines that got emitted by

each run and it prints that number *minus* 1 to ignore the last
line that always reads:

```
9 9 9 array elements:   60
```

The final step pipes the output of each iteration from the
'`for-do-done`' loop into yet another small bit of AWK to
count up the number of each '`n-1`' value that gets emitted
from all those runs.

The '`END`' action displays the output line counts ('0', '1', '2',
'3', '...') with the frequency of occurrence of those number
of output lines — where the array element value was greater
than `0.95`.

The following list of output shows the line counts with
observed frequency of occurrence in the results I got from my
twenty (20) minute run of the 1000 iterations at 1.2 seconds
apart:

```
0 47
1 152
2 204
3 239
4 183
5 97
6 53
7 15
8 9
9 1


real      20m13.374s
user      0m7.894s
sys       0m11.468s
```

The output from the '`time`' command reports the expected
elapsed (**real**) time of 20 minutes and 13 seconds.

The actual run time of the 1000 repetitions of the AWK
process was a matter of seconds — most of the time got
taken up waiting for the sleep processes to time out between
each run — because I wanted to ensure there should be a
different seed value given to the random number generator
calls made to 'rand()'.

Next I searched my 'python' source code area for a script
to help me plot these data values and after one or two edits
came up with this:

```python
#!/usr/bin/python2
# Program:  x-y-stem-plot.py
#    Usage:  $ ./x-y-stem-plot.py
# Purpose:
#    Read two (2) columns of data from
#    input file "x-y.txt" into "numpy"
#    arrays 'x' and 'y' for plotting
#    as a "matplotlib.pyplot.stem"
#    style plot diagram.
#
import sys
import numpy as np
import matplotlib.pyplot as plt
x, y = np.loadtxt('x-y.txt', delimiter=' ',
         usecols=(0,1), unpack=True)
plt.stem(x, y)
plt.show()
```

Note: Although I use 'python3' I needed to use 'python2'
because there was a mis-match between my versions of the
'numpy' and 'matplotlib' libraries.

Here is the 'stem' plot diagram produced from the results
data listed above:

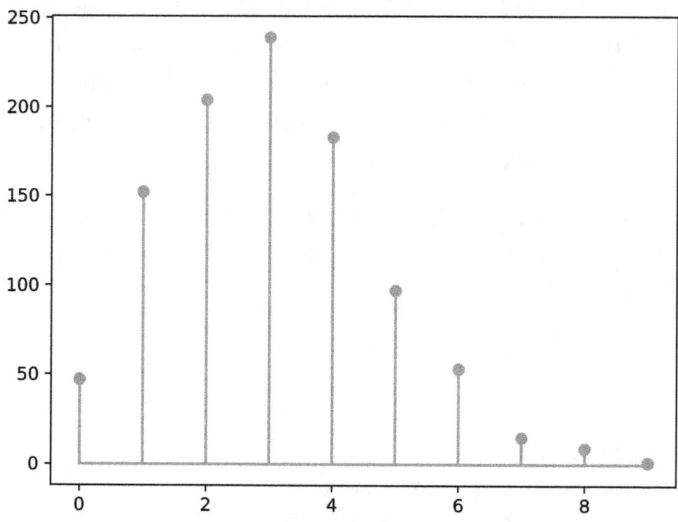

The horizontal axis shows the number of lines of output for array values greater than 0.95 and the vertical axis shows frequency of occurrence of the number of times that line count got observed during the 1000 sample runs I made of the AWK code.

I was expecting the slight positive skew in the data distribution with the hint of a longer tail on the right side in the plot diagram.

The interesting surprise was to see the 47 frequency count for zero output lines. On reflection, of course, this is well within the bounds of statistical probabilities.

An interesting exercise that took about half a day to write bits of code, dig out an old python plotting script and make modifications to that for the 'stem' style plot and then save the plots to files and find commands to convert color plot images into monochrome or gray scale images for inclusion in both my paper book and 'epub' document versions.

3.8 Special file names

AWK lets us use three different special file names:
'/dev/stdin', '/dev/stdout' and '/dev/stderr' with
commands like 'getline' for input and commands like
'print' and 'printf' for output:

```
print "Error:  text ..." > "/dev/stderr"
```

The 'Error: text ...' will appear on our interactive
terminal for us to see and deal with. Other 'print'
statements that write to the standard output stream could
get redirected into another file that does not contain any
error or *warning* message(s) — if we choose.

3.9 User defined functions

User defined functions in AWK get specified with code that
looks like this:

```
function name(paramList) {
    statements }
```

These can be stand-alone functions we use in one AWK
script — or they could get encapsulated into a *library* file of
functions we can call from within other AWK scripts.

Notes:

1. Functions can call each other and can use recursion
   (call themselves)

2. Functions can include 'return' statement(s) to return
   control to the point from which they got called

3. A '**return** *expr*' statement can return a value (the result of '*expr*') to the calling point if necessary

4. The return value remains undefined if we do not specify one — or if the function returns — as it will when it reaches the end of it's formal definition at its final right curly brace '}' character

5. When calling a function the left parenthesis character '(' must be touching the function name — without any blank space

6. The *paramList* is a list of zero or more comma separated variable names with a special quality — these items act like "*local*" variables within the body of the function — with one exception — arrays,

7. Scalar variables (numbers, strings) get passed in by *value* — any changes we make remain within the function code

8. Array variables get passed in by *reference* — any changes we make to arrays get made to the array in the calling code's "*global*" namespace

Caveat Any variable used in a function that is *not* named in the function's parameter list is visible and accessible in the global program's namespace.

Any variable in the parameter list for which no value gets supplied when the function gets called stays as a local variable in the function and has no initial value.

By convention we put a comma and three or four blank spaces after the function's list of expected call parameters and then nominate any function private local variable(s) before the closing right parenthesis character:

```
function new(a, b,    p, q) {
```

```
        # a & b get passed in for use
        # p & q remain as local vars
        ...
    }

    new(9, "scalar")
```

In general, any changes we make to scalar variables inside our
functions should remain inside those functions — provided
we have named those identifiers in the parameter list on the
right — after the real function call parameters.

It took me a year or two to get my head around the relevance
of that — I'm a bit slow!

A section headed 'USER-DEFINED FUNCTIONS' in 'man gawk'
explains these rather well.

3.10   User function libraries

The GNU 'gawk' command includes command-line options
and arguments to help us include the AWK code we store in
other files. For example:

```
    gawk -f myprog mydata
```

Or:

```
    gawk --include mylib -f myprog mydata
```

gawk will concatenate all the AWK code it finds in the
included file ('mylib') and the specified program file
('myprog').

Next it will begin reading input data records from 'mydata'
— or from *standard input* if we use a dash (-) as the input
file name and then take the specified *action(s)*.

The library code could also get included by using a program
code statement like:

```
@include "/path/to/mylib"
```

If we don't specify the absolute '/path/to/' part then
AWK will first check the *current* run directory ('.') or the
'/usr/local/share/awk' directory for the specified 'mylib'
file (or whatever name we have used).

gawk will also look for shell environment variables named
'AWKPATH' and 'AWKLIBPATH' that we can define to help the
AWK code locate our program source and library files if we
want to store those somewhere else.

For more details we can search for those variable names in
the on-line information in:

```
man gawk
```

3.11   Scalar and array parameters

Here's an example exploring the difference between scalar and
array parameters that we pass into and/or access within our
own functions:

```
# fun.awk --> testing AWK
#     function parameters
BEGIN { ary[1] = 11; ary[2] = 22;
    ary[3] = 33; p = "|"
    s = 3; u = 44 }
function fun1(a) {
    print "enter:  array a:",
       a[1], p, a[2], p, a[3]
    delete a[2]
    a[3] = "wow"
```

```awk
        print "leave:  array a:",
            a[1], p, a[2], p, a[3]
}
function fun2(s, t) {
        print "enter:  s, t, u:",
            s, p, t, p, u
        s = s * t
        t = t + 5
        u = u * 2
        print "leave:  s, t, u:",
            s, p, t, p, u
}
{
        print "1.  start array ary:",
            ary[1], p, ary[2], p, ary[3]
        print "call function fun1(ary)",
            "--> (a)"
        fun1(a)
        print ""
        print "2.  start scalars s, t, u:",
            s, p, t, p, u
        print "call function fun2(s, 3)",
            "--> (s, t)"
        fun2(s, 3)
}
END {
        print ""
        print "3.  End results:"
        print "final:  array ary:",
            ary[1], p, ary[2], p, ary[3]
        print "final:  scalars s, t, u:",
            s, p, t, p, u
}
```

When this gets run:

```
$ echo | awk -f fun.awk -
```

```
1.    start array ary:    11 | 22 | 33
call function fun1(ary) --> (a)
enter:   array:   a:    11 | 22 | 33
leave:   array:   a:    11 |    | wow

2.    start scalars s, t, u:   2 |   | 44
call function fun2(s, 3) --> (s, t)
enter:   s, t, u:   2 | 3 | 44
leave:   s, t, u:   6 | 8 | 88

3.    End results:
final:   array ary:   11 |    | wow
final:   scalars s, t, u:   2 |   | 88
```

Notes:

1. The 'BEGIN' *pattern* sets initial values for three
   elements in *array* 'a' and three scalar variables named
   'p', 's' and 'u'

2. In function 'fun1' the parameter 'a' is an array that
   gets passed in by *reference* — anything we do to 'a' in
   this function will *change* the values in the array ('ary')
   that got passed in — like deleting an element or setting
   an element to 'wow'

3. In function 'fun2' we pass in two scalar variables: 's'
   and 't' — these get passed in by *value* and we then
   change the values of those inside the function — we also
   use a variable called 'u' that we did not pass in as a
   parameter — is this a *local* variable inside the function?

4. Look at the variable named 'u' that got set to a value
   of '44' in the 'BEGIN' area — it got affected by the 2
   times multiplication inside function 'fun2' and now has
   a final value of '88'

5. Local variables inside a function need to get mentioned
   at the end of the parameter list — unless we use

new name identifiers we have not used in the main
namespace — its better to use the method for
specifying function local variables already outlined
above — add a comma and blank spaces and then list
each of the function local variables in the extended
parameter list

6. When blank spaces appear between the pipe ('|')
   symbols in the output text — this indicates there was
   a missing or undefined variable — like 't' in the main
   action area — or array element 'ary[2]' after it gets
   deleted as 'a[2]' inside function 'fun1'

At times we could need to take these unusual language
implementation features into consideration to help unravel
the reason why a piece of code doesn't operate in the way we
think it should.

AWK will always do what we ask it to do — that might not
be what we imagined.

Computer programming is a fascinating subject.

Exercise 3.1 What change in the definition for function
'fun2' could prevent the change observed in the external
variable 'u' ?

Chapter 4

Making use of gawk

Other than our own imagination — there's not much that can limit the ways we can press AWK into usable service for us at one time or another.

If we can think of a computing task — especially in the area of text and data processing that we need to achieve — it's often easy to think about ways in which AWK can help.

4.1   Gawk in a bash script

The following example shows one way to use AWK code inside a small 'bash' script wrapper to make it easy to run the AWK functionality like any other Linux command we use in 'bash' scripts.

```
#!/usr/bin/bash
# corf --> convert degrees C or F
# Usage:  echo 22.5c | ./corf # C to F
#    Or:  echo 75 F | ./corf  # F to C
#    Or:  echo 45cf | ./corf # (Both)
#    Or:  cat temps.txt | ./corf
```

```
    awk '
    /[Cc]/ { dCi = $1+0
        dFo = sprintf("%0.2f", (dCi*9/5+32))
            print dCi, "degC is", dFo, "degF"
    }
    /[Ff]/ { dFi = $1+0
        dCo = sprintf("%0.2f", (dFi-32)*5/9)
            print dFi, "degF is", dCo, "degC"
    } -
```

The first line is the 'hash-bang-bin-bash' line and tells our
interactive or other shell process to use the '/usr/bin/bash'
process to start interpreting the content in this file.

Other lines that start with a cross-hatch or *hash* character
('#') are comments for our own information.

Next the 'awk' (or '/usr/bin/gawk' interpreter will get run
to interpret the rest of the code to perform the *actions* we
request for each of the two defined *patterns* .

The AWK code wants a number (of degrees) followed by a 'C'
and/or an 'F' character(s) — both UPPER case or lower case
scale designators get accepted in the two regular expression
character patterns '/[Cc]/' and '/[Ff]/'.

Note: We can specify *both* letters ('c' and 'f') if we want the
two alternatives evaluated.

Based on the pattern selection the code will calculate the
conversion from the entered temperature scale and prints
out the input value and the output value in the other
temperature scale.

A Google search in November 2025 reported there is still 19
countries who make use of the Fahrenheit temperature scale
— the USA, Cayman Islands, Liberia, the Marshall Islands
and Micronesia for some.

Use your favourite text editor (like 'vim'?) to add those lines

of code into a file called 'corf' or any other name you choose
— and then make the file executable by running the Linux
command:

```
$ chmod 700 corf
```

The 'corf' script can get run like this:

```
$ echo 32.5c | ./corf
32.5 degC is 90.50 degF
```

Or:

```
$ echo 100f | ./corf
100 degF is 37.78 degC
```

Or even if we want both results:

```
$ echo 40cf | ./corf
40 degC is 104.00 degF
40 degF is 4.44 degC
```

Both of the regular expression patterns get evaluated as true
and the corresponding action(s) get run for each one.

Another way to use the script is with an input file containing
temperature values and the scale designators — one on each
line — for example:

```
$ cat temps.txt
22c
25.5C
32cf
40c
65f
72f
```

```
90F
115f
212F
```

We can use the 'cat' command to feed these data lines into the './corf' script:

```
$ cat temps.txt | ./corf
22 degC is 71.60 degF
25.5 degC is 77.90 degF
32 degC is 89.60 degF
32 degF is 0.00 degC
40 degC is 104.00 degF
65 degF is 18.33 degC
75 degF is 23.89 degC
90 degF is 32.22 degC
115 degF is 46.11 degC
212 degF is 100.00 degC
```

The results appear accurate enough for general purposes.

If more accuracy is necessary the "%0.2f" terms in the calls to the 'sprintf' function could get adjusted to "%0.4f" or "%0.6f", etc.

4.2   Gawk at number totals

Suppose we have a large cluttered directory and we want to count the total number of files it contains — or the total number of bytes contained in all those files.

I like to use the 'ls -go' command to display a list of file system objects in my Linux terminals — it leaves out the user and group ownership fields and means the output looks a bit like this:

```
$ ls -go | head
total 19212
-rw-r-----  1   67 Jun 26 15:20 123.txt
drwxr-x---  2 4096 Jan 26  2024 1st-dots
drwxr-x---  3 4096 Jun 13 12:09 AAA
drwxr-x---  3 4096 May 19  2024 AAAAA
-rw-r-----  1  276 Sep 16  2024 ab.csv
drwxr-x--- 63 4096 Sep 15 09:55 apps
-rw-r-----  1 7396 Feb 13  2024 awk.txt
drwxr-x---  3 4096 Sep 29 10:58 BBB
-rw-r-----  1  369 Dec  7  2023 b.tex
...
```

Gak! There's an accumulation of all kinds of files and
directories.

Lines that commence with a dash ('-') are files — lines that
commence with a 'd' are directories.

In the 'ls -go' output the numbers in column 2 are file
system object link counts — for most files this number is '1'
unless we use lots of links to files for some reason.

Directory entries have at least two links — for the current
('.') and parent ('..') directories plus another one for each
sub-directory.

In the 'ls -go' output the numbers in column 3 give the file
system object size in bytes.

We can use AWK with the regular expression constant
pattern '/^-/' to match the lines for each 'file' entry in the
lines that begin with a dash ('-') character.

This helps us to *ignore* the first output line that contains the
'total' number of links reported by the 'ls -go' command.

In the data that gets matched or selected by AWK — the
summation of the file link numbers displayed in column 'n=2'
or the file byte sizes displayed in column 'n=3' will provide

two numbers for use in further assessment:

```
$ ls -go | awk '/^-/ {
    nml = nml+1
    ttl = ttl+($n+0)
}
END {
    print "matched lines in:", nml
    if (n == 2) str = "links:"
    if (n == 3) str = "bytes:"
    print "total file", str, ttl
}' n=2 -
matched lines in:   335
total file links:   335
```

The 'n=2' argument passed into AWK before the trailing
dash ('-') — the read from standard input specifier — sets
the variable 'n' to the value '2' and this gets used in the
summation of 'ttl' (the *total*) using the numeric values of
the input field ('$n+0') found on each matching input data
line in the specified column number.

Counting up the total number of bytes in column '3' by using
an argument 'n=3' with AWK will display the total number
of bytes in all those files:

```
$ ls -go | awk '/^-/ {
    nml = nml+1
    ttl = ttl+($n+0)
}
END {
    print "matched lines in:", nml
    if (n == 2) str = "links:"
    if (n == 3) str = "bytes:"
    print "total file", str, ttl
}' n=3 -
```

```
matched lines in:   335
total file bytes:   120205813
```

Over 115 megabytes in 335 files!

Mea culpa — it must be time for a big tidy up — after I get this book finished.

Exercise 4.1: Add a 'hash-bang-bin-bash' line and that chunk of AWK code into an executable file named like 'my-files.sh' and make modifications to get it to display *both* the 'total file links:' and the 'total file bytes:' in one run.

Exercise 4.2: Add an extra '*pattern*' with an '*action*' to count the number of directory entries and display that extra information too.

4.3   Gawk at counting words

On page 119 of "*The AWK Programming Language*" book there's a clever piece of AWK code called 'wordfreq'. I hope the authors will not mind me showing you an approximation to their published code:

```
# wordfreq - print number of
#    occurrences of each word
{
    # remove most punctuation:
    gsub(/[.,:;!?(){}]/, "")
    for (i=1; i<=NF; i==)
        count[$i]++
}
END { for (w in count)
    print count[w], w | "sort -rn"
}
```

Notice in the second last line how the script pipes the stream of '`print count[w], w`' result lines into the Linux '`sort`' utility with options '`-rn`' to get *reverse numeric* order.

If we make a small file called '`wordfreq`' containing those lines of AWK code then we can run the program on a text file named '`file.txt`' like this:

```
$ awk -f wordfreq file.txt
```

Or we could count word frequencies in the '`gawk`' on line manual page and look at the first ten (10) entries by running:

```
$ man gawk | awk -f wordfreq - | head
842 the
345 of
297 is
293 a
274 to
242 and
218 in
207 The
167 are
136 for
```

You could pipe the output into '`less`' to see more entries in a manageable output.

The output will contain a list of lines with two items on each — the word *counts* and the *word* for each of the strings it considers as a word.

Not perfect for all types of text — it's a good starting point to help you build your own word frequency tool.

Exercise 4.3 Change the code in '`wordfreq`' so that words like '`the`' and '`The`' get counted together instead of separately.

4.4   Gawk at text format

On the page after the 'wordfreq' program in *"The AWK Programming Language"* book there's another elegant piece of code I think everyone deserves to see:

```
# fmt.awk --> format plain text input
# Usage:  awk -f fmt.awk [wid={nn}] file
BEGIN { wid = 64 }
/./  { for (i=1; i<=NF; i++) addword($i) }
/^$/ { printline(); print "" }
END  { printline() }
function addword(w) {
    if (length(line) + length(w) > wid)
        printline()
    line = line " " w
}
function printline() {
    if (length(line) > 0) {
        # remove leading blank
        print substr(line, 2)
        line = ""
    }
}
```

If we have a plain text file that needs to get reformatted to shorter lines — say 64 characters wide — we can run this super AWK script like this:

```
$ awk -f fmt.awk infile > out.txt
```

If you prefer your lines of text a little wider — or not that wide — we can add a definition for the 'wid' variable it uses for the output line width:

```
$ awk -f fmt.awk wid=72 infile > out.txt
```

Here's a quick test to show what to expect:

```
$ man gawk > gawk.txt
$ awk -f fmt.awk gawk.txt > gawk-64.txt
$ ls -go gawk*.txt
-rw-r----- 1 82793 Nov 8 19:03 gawk-64.txt
-rw-r----- 1 108622 Nov 8 19:03 gawk.txt
$ wc gawk*.txt
2006 13590 82793 gawk-64.txt
2191 13590 108622 gawk.txt
4197 27180 191415 total
```

The 'ls -go' command reports the two 'gawk*.txt' files
have a different size. Did we lose some text?

The 'wc' (*word-count*) command reports the number of word
in each of those files in the second column of the two lines
before the 'total' output line. These are identical: '13590'
words — no we didn't lose any word text — we did reduce
and re-arrange the blank spaces.

I find the result particularly pleasing.

I deplore trying to read long lines of text that stretch for
over more than about 70 character. I find my eyes and brain
appreciate shorter lines.

Now there's a simple way to get those.

4.5   Gawk at re-ordering fields

Data files come in all shaped and sizes.

At times we could have other programs that require our data
to appear in a certain column order for plotting in an (x, y)
co-ordinate graph — or when we have ten columns of data
and we need to extract columns five and two — in that order.

Here is an example of a bash shell with AWK code to help
re-organise columns of data when we need that:

```bash
#!/usr/bin/bash
# Program:  fld-reord.sh; re-order fields
# Usage:  fld-reord.sh infl fld,lst
# Or:  cat infl | fld-reord.sh '-' fld,lst
if [ $# -ne 2 ] ; then
    echo "Usage:  fld-reord.sh infl f,lst"
    echo "Or:  cat infl | fld-reord.sh '-'
f,lst"
    exit 1
fi
infl="$1" ; flst="$2"
awk 'NR < 2 {
    n = split(ford, ord, ",")
}
{

    printf "%s", $ord[1]
    for (i=2; i<=n; i++) {
        printf " %s", $ord[i]
    } print ""
}' ford="$flst" "$infl"
```

What does the script do?

It starts with the expected 'hash-bang-bin-bash' line to tell
the Linux system how to interpret the code.

Lines that begin with a cross-hatch or hash ('#') character
are comments for human consumption.

The next five lines describe a conditional 'if-then-fi'
statement to display a 'Usage:' message if the script gets
called without two (2) arguments — and then it exits back
to the calling shell with an error value of '1' — meaning it's
un-successful.

If two arguments did get used then we hope these are the
input file name and a comma separated list of field numbers

in the order the user wants to extract.

The next line assigns the values of those two run-time arguments to two shell variables for later use on the last line of the script.

The next line runs the AWK interpreter with a starting *pattern* of:

```
NR == 1
```

to get run at the time when AWK reads its first line of input. The action performed is to 'split' a variable named 'ford' (*mnemonic* for 'field order') — and using a comma (',')separator into an array called 'ord' (*mnemonic* for the 'order') and return 'n' — the number of such fields to get re-ordered.

In the next *action* part that has no pattern matching — and will get run on every line of input data (including the first line) — the code will print out the data fields in the order requested by the script user.

The last line is where those two run-time arguments get fed into the AWK process as variable 'ford' and the input file name.

We could have a ghastly data file named 'tst.txt' with a content that looks like this:

```
$ cat tst.txt
1 2 3 4 5 6 7 8 9 10 11 12
i ii iii iv v vi vii viii ix
1.  2.  3.  4.  5.  6.  7.  8.  9.
f1 f2 f3 f4 f5 f6 f6 f7 f8
```

— that's okay as long as the field separators match what AWK is expecting.

Running the 'fld-reord.sh' script to extract fields five
(5) and three (3) and emit them in that order can get
accomplished with relative ease — here is what the output
could look like when running on this set of data:

```
$ ./fld-reord.sh tst.txt 5,3
5 3
v iii
5.  3.
f5 f3
```

4.6   Gawk at array rotation

One day a physicist I worked with asked: *"Can I get you to
rotate a 2D array of data points please?"*

My unvoiced internal response was *"Gak!"*

I sheepishly replied: *"Give me a while and I'll see what I can
do."*

I went back to my desk and considered the problem and then
thought: *"This sounds like a task for the AWK interpreter!"*

An hour or two later I'd written this code and saved it into a
bash shell wrapper named 'rot8ary.sh':

```
#!/bin/bash
# Program:  rot8ary.sh --> rotate rows
# and columns of a 2D data array
# Usage:  rot8ary.sh inp.dat > out.dat
inFil="$1"
awk 'BEGIN { cmax = 0 ; rmax = 0 }
# Read "rows" of data and store the
# values in 2D array "ary[row,col]":
{
    rmax++
```

```
            if (NF > cmax) cmax = NF
            for (i=1; i <= NF; i++) {
                ary[rmax,i] = $i
            }
        }
        END {
            # Loop over columns:
            for (i=1; i <= cmax; i++) {
                printf "%s", ary[rmax,i]
                # Reverse loop over rows:
                for (j=rmax-1; j >= 1; j--) {
                    if (ary[j,i] != "") {
                        printf " %s", ary[j,i]
                    } else {
                        printf " ."
                    }
                }
                print ""
            }
        }' "$inFil"
```

To test this I used a small set of sample data in a file named
'in.dat':

```
11 12 13 14
21 22 23 24
31 32 33 34
```

Next I ran this through the AWK code with the Linux
command:

```
$ rot8ary.sh in.dat > out1.dat
```

The result was this:

```
$ cat out1.dat
```

```
31 21 11
32 22 12
33 23 13
34 24 14
```

Next I called the program three more times:

```
$ rot8ary.sh out1.dat > out2.dat
$ rot8ary.sh out2.dat > out3.dat
$ rot8ary.sh out3.dat > out4.dat
```

Then compared the starting file with the 4th rotation:

```
$ cmp in.dat out4.dat
# No news is good news!
```

The final file contained:

```
11 12 13 14
21 22 23 24
31 32 33 34
```

I knocked on the physicist's door and handed him a page
with a brief note about how to run the program.

"That was quick" was his surprised reply. *"Always a
pleasure"* was mine.

Later in the day he showed me a plot diagram he'd managed
to produce from his rotated arrays of data.

Another happy customer!

The input file and output files for each of the four rotate
operations I used in my testing were these:

```
$ cat in.dat
```

```
11 12 13 14
21 22 23 24
31 32 33 34

$ for i in 1 2 3 4 ; do
> cat out$i.dat
> echo
> done
31 21 11
32 22 12
33 23 13
34 24 14

34 33 32 31
24 23 22 21
14 13 12 11

14 24 34
13 23 33
12 22 32
11 21 31

11 12 13 14
21 22 23 24
31 32 33 34
```

What would I have done without an AWK interpreter?

I might have needed to write a bit of C++ code to do more
or less the same thing — but then getting the data in and
out might have caused me some angst.

Chapter 5

Answers to exercises

Exercise 3.1

The change in the definition for function 'fun2' to prevent
the external change to variable 'u' is the simple addition in
the first line of 'fun2':

```
function fun2(s, t,    u) {
    ...
}
```

Putting 'u' at the right-hand end of the list of parameters
signifies this is another variable we want to keep as *local*
within the function.

We still call the function with two input arguments like:

```
fun2(s, 3)
```

Even though there's a variable named 'u' in the global
namespace — any use of variable 'u' inside the function will
remain hidden from the external one.

Here is the output again with that one change made to the
'fun2' parameter list:

```
$ echo | awk -f fun-2.awk -
1.  start array ary:  11 | 22 | 33
call function fun1(ary) --> (a)
enter:  array a:  11 | 22 | 33
leave:  array a:  11 | | wow

2.  start scalars s, t, u:  2 | | 44
call function fun2(s, 3) --> (s, t)
enter:  s, t, u:  2 | 3 |
leave:  s, t, u:  6 | 8 | 0

3.  End results:
final:  array ary:  11 | | wow
final:  scalars s, t, u:  2 | | 44
```

Notice what's changed?

The "`enter:  s, t, u:  2 | 3 |` " line now has no value
for 'u' because that was not yet set inside '`fun2`' at that
point.

The "`leave:  s, t, u:  6 | 8 | 0`" line displays a value
of zero ('0') for 'u' because nothing (an *unset* 'u' variable)
multiplied by '2' is still nothing — coerced to the number '0'.

The "`final:  scalars s, t, u:  2 | | 44`" line displays
the expected value of '44' for the global namespace variable
'u' because we added 'u' at the right-hand end of the
parameter list in the definition for function '`fun2`' to keep
the function's use of 'u' local within the scope of the function.

Exercise 4.1:

Here's one way to get both the '`file links`' and the '`files
bytes`' totals for the files in a directory in one run:

```
#!/usr/bin/bash
# Program:  my-files.sh
```

```
# Usage:  cd {dir} ; ./my-files.sh
ls -go | awk '/^-/ {
    # nml --> number of matched lines
    nml = nml+1
    # c2ttl --> col.2 numbers total
    c2ttl = c2ttl+($2+0)
    # c3ttl --> col.3 numbers total
    c3ttl = c3ttl+($3+0)
}
END {
    print "matched in lines:", nml
    print "total file links:", c2ttl
    print "total file bytes:", c3ttl
}' -
```

Running this code in that same cluttered directory gives me
the expected result:

```
$ ./my-files.sh
matched in lines:   335
total file links:   335
total file bytes:   120205813
```

Exercise 4.2:

In the 'ls -go' output the directory entries start with a
letter 'd' at the left side. One way to add another *pattern* to
match those and print their total number is like this:

```
#!/usr/bin/bash
# Program:  my-files.sh
# Usage:  cd {dir} ; my-files.sh
ls -go | awk '
/^d/ {
    # nde --> num directory entries
```

```
        nde = nde + 1
    }
    /^-/ {
        # nfe --> number of file entries
        nfe = nfe + 1
        # c2ttl --> col.2 numbers total
        c2ttl = c2ttl+($2+0)
        # c3ttl --> col.3 numbers total
        c3ttl = c3ttl+($3+0)
    }
    END {
        print "total directories:", nde
        print "total file lines.:", nfe
        print "total file links.:", c2ttl
        print "total file bytes.:", c3ttl
    }' -
```

Running this modified code in that same cluttered directory gives me the added directory information:

```
$ ./my-files.sh
total directories:   145
total file lines.:   335
total file links.:   335
total file bytes.:   120205813
```

The tidy up task before me could be bigger than I imagined — it will keep me quiet for a while.

Exercise 4.3:

The original 'wordfreq' code looked like this:

```
# wordfreq --> Print number of
#   occurrences of each word
{
```

```
    # Remove most punctuation:
    gsub(/[.,:;!?()]/, "")
    for (i=1; i<=NF; i==)
      count[$i]++
}
END { for (w in count)
    print count[w], w | "sort -rn"
}
```

A small modification to the 'wordfreq' code — changing this
line:

```
count[$i]++
```

into this:

```
count[tolower($i)]++
```

is all that's required to combine the UPPER case and lower
case words like 'The' and 'the'.

Note: Before I had heard of the GNU 'toupper()' and
'tolower()' functions in 'gawk' I had written my own slower
implementation in a function I called 'fnUc2lc':

```
    # fnUc2lc --> Convert UPPER case
    #   to lower case in input "str"
    # Return:  all lower case string
    function fnUc2lc(str,    AZ,az,i,lc,UC) {
        AZ = "ABCDEFGHIJKLMNOPQRSTUVWXYZ"
        az = "abcdefghijklmnopqrstuvwxyz"
        for (i = 1; i <= 26; i++) {
          UC = substr(AZ,i,1)
          lc = substr(az,i,1)
          gsub(UC, lc, str)
        }
        return str
    }
```

I used the Linux 'time' utility to measure the difference in speed between the newer gawk 'tolower()' function and my old 'fnUc2lc()' function. The results were:

```
tolower() --> 0.070 seconds
fnUc2lc() --> 0.335 seconds
```

My old function is about five times slower than 'tolower()':

```
0.335 / 0.070 = 4.786
```

This is a function I wrote that did not work as I had hoped and expected until *after* I realised the importance of naming *all* of a function's internal (*local*) variables in that right-hand part of the parameter list.

I had tried to use an early version of function 'fnUc2lc' in other AWK programs that had already used a variable named 'i' in a global action area like that 'for' loop: "for(i=1;i<=NF;i==)" in the "wordfreq" code.

We live and we learn — I've already said — I'm a bit slow!

I hope you have enjoyed taking a gawk at some of the capabilities of AWK.

Now, I have some tidying up work to do in that cluttered directory.

By the same author

Nonfiction

Epub

God redeems the reject
Recounts how the author, the reject, received the precious gift from God that Jesus called — *"the promise of the Father"*
2025, ISBN 9781764299725

9 dozen 9 character word puzzles
9 dozen 9 character word puzzles says it all
2025, ISBN 9781764299701

Linux Clues
Tips and clues about using the Linux operating system
2025, ISBN 9781764057882

The Miracle Working God
Describes God's miracle working activity in my life
2025, ISBN 9781764057868

Love, Joy, Peace

Living a better life by the Grace of God
2025, ISBN 9791764057844

Glory to God Everywhere You Are There
Describes the origins of my simple song of praise
2025, ISBN 9781764057820

Jesus Says You Must Be Born Again
The most important information the world affords
2025, ISBN 9781764057813

Nonfiction

Paperback

God redeems the reject
Recounts how the author, the reject, received the precious gift from God that Jesus called — *"the promise of the Father"*
2025, ISBN 9781764299732

9 dozen 9 character word puzzles
9 dozen 9 character word puzzles says it all
2025, ISBN 9781764299718

Linux Clues
Tips and clues about using the Linux operating system
2025, ISBN 9781764057899

The Miracle Working God
Describes God's miracle working activity in my life
2025, ISBN 9781764057875

Love, Joy, Peace
Living a better life by the Grace of God
2025, ISBN 9791764057851

Glory to God Everywhere You Are There
Describes the origins of my simple song of praise
2025, ISBN 9781764057837

Jesus Says You Must Be Born Again
The most important information the world affords
2025, ISBN 9781764057806

Paul's Question
Have you received the Holy Spirit?
2023, ISBN 9798857128381

Linux Bread Crumbs
Learn to use Linux
2023, ISBN 9798364005830

To Day If You Will Hear His Voice
Believe in God
2022, ISBN 9798831130669

Take Another Look
Please take another look
2022, ISBN 9798437605554

Song Lyrics
Notes and lyrics for 16 of my songs
2022, ISBN 9798434494120

Fiction

Paperback

The Ravenscroft Algorithm
Fictitious cyber crime
2022, ISBN 9798842106202

Broke Reef
Fictitious shipwreck on a W.Aust. Reef
2022, ISBN 9798428316940